FX!
Computer-Generated Imagery

Timothy J. Bradley

Consultants

Timothy Rasinski, Ph.D.
Kent State University

Lori Oczkus, M.A.
Literacy Consultant

Publishing Credits

Rachelle Cracchiolo, M.S.Ed., *Publisher*

Conni Medina, M.A.Ed., *Managing Editor*

Dona Herweck Rice, *Series Developer*

Emily R. Smith, M.A.Ed., *Content Director*

Stephanie Bernard/Susan Daddis, M.A.Ed., *Editors*

Robin Erickson, *Senior Graphic Designer*

The TIME logo is a registered trademark of TIME Inc. Used under license.

Image Credits: Cover and p.1 Universal Pictures/AF Archive/Alamy Stock Photo; p.5 Marsyas, used under Creative Commons BY-SA 3.0; p.6 TriStar Pictures/AF Archive/Alamy Stock Photo; pp.8–9 20th Century Fox/AF Archive/Alamy Stock Photo; p.11 Dan Tuffs/Getty Images; p.15 Collection Christophel/Alamy Stock Photo; p.16 Warner Bros./AF archive/Alamy Stock Photo; pp.18–19 Hitoshi Yamada/ZUMA Press/Newscom; p.20 Moviestore collection Ltd/Alamy Stock Photo; pp.21 and back cover Collection Christophel/Alamy Stock Photo; p.22 Moviestore Collection Ltd/Alamy Stock Photo; p.24 Touchstone Pictures/AF archive/Alamy Stock Photo; p.26 Paramount Pictures/AF archive/Alamy Stock Photo; pp.28–29 Illustration by Timothy J. Bradley; p.30 Universal Pictures/Photos 12 /Alamy Stock Photo; p.31 Universal Pictures/Pictorial Press Ltd/Alamy Stock Photo; p.32 20th Century Fox/AF archive/Alamy Stock Photo; p.33 Photos 12/ Alamy Stock Photo; p.34 Pictorial Press Ltd/Alamy Stock Photo; p.35 Warner Bros./AF archive/ Alamy Stock Photo; p.36 Moviestore collection Ltd/Alamy Stock Photo; p.37 AF archive/Alamy Stock Photo; p.44 age fotostock/Alamy Stock Photo; pp.46, 47 AF archive/Alamy Stock Photo; p.50 (top) GongTo/Shutterstock.com, (bottom) s_bukley/Shutterstock.com; p.51 (top and bottom) Featureflash Photo Agency/Shutterstock.com, (middle) Joe Seer/Shutterstock.com; p.52 (top) Michael Tullberg/Getty Images, (middle) s_bukley/Shutterstock.com, (bottom) ZUMA Press, Inc./ Alamy Stock Photo; p.53 (top) Featureflash Photo Agency/Shutterstock.com, (middle) Presselect/ Alamy Stock Photo, (bottom) Tinseltown/Shutterstock.com; pp.54–55 Alexander Tolstykh/Alamy Stock Photo; p.56 Dikiiy/Shutterstock.com; all other images from iStock and/or Shutterstock.

Notes: Readers should have parental permission before viewing movies in this book due to possible mature theme or images. All characters are trademarks of their respective owners or developers and are used in this book strictly for editorial purposes. No commercial claim to their use is made by the author or publisher.

Library of Congress Cataloging-in-Publication Data

Names: Bradley, Timothy J., author.
Title: FX! : computer-generated imagery / Timothy J. Bradley.
Description: Huntington Beach, CA : Teacher Created Materials, [2017] | Includes index. | Audience: Grades 7-8.
Identifiers: LCCN 2016034990 (print) | LCCN 2016036292 (ebook) | ISBN 9781493836147 (pbk.) | ISBN 9781480757189 (eBook)
Subjects: LCSH: Digital cinematography--Juvenile literature. | Cinematography--Special effects--Juvenile literature.
Classification: LCC TR860 .B68 2017 (print) | LCC TR860 (ebook) | DDC 777/.9--dc23
LC record available at https://lccn.loc.gov/2016034990

Teacher Created Materials

5301 Oceanus Drive
Huntington Beach, CA 92649-1030
http://www.tcmpub.com

ISBN 978-1-4938-3614-7

© 2017 Teacher Created Materials, Inc.
Printed in China
Nordica.082019.CA21901021

Table of Contents

Crafting a Blockbuster

Imagine you're a film director, and you've just been handed a script for a blockbuster film. The script calls for giant spaceships, creepy alien invaders, and fierce space battles. How can you possibly create all those **special effects**, and *more*, in time for a summer **release**?

Computers! Whatever a story needs, computers can deliver eye-popping visuals to make your movie look awesome. Magical creatures? No problem. Huge, detailed space battle? Of course! Robot invasion of planet Earth? You've got it! With the right **hardware**, **software**, and artists, filmmakers can create dazzling visual effects for their movies. They do this through computer-generated imagery, or CGI. This gives directors the freedom to bring to life anything they can imagine.

Blockbuster

The word *blockbuster* has been used since the 1920s. But it wasn't until the 1970s, when films such as *Jaws* and *Star Wars* were released, that it became a popular way to describe hit movies.

It all starts with amazing computer technology. The first "computer" was invented in the second century BC in Greece and was used to calculate planetary movements through the **cosmos**. Little did anyone know that computers would evolve to become an integral part of our everyday lives.

AntiKythera Mechanism, believed to be the first "computer"

Computers help operate cars, phones, and homes. They allow us to play games, explore the world and the universe, and create astounding film effects that keep audiences enthralled and lining up for more.

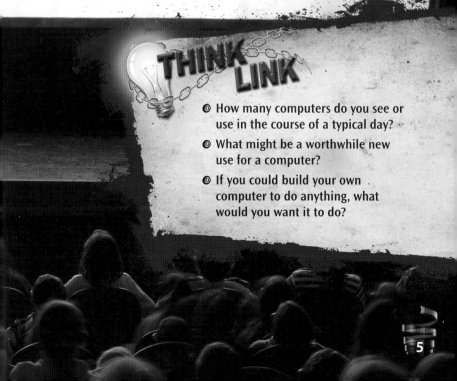

THINK LINK

- ◉ How many computers do you see or use in the course of a typical day?
- ◉ What might be a worthwhile new use for a computer?
- ◉ If you could build your own computer to do anything, what would you want it to do?

"Old School" Special Effects

Until about thirty years ago, special effects in film and television were created using **practical effects**. Models of spacecrafts and cities with puppets are examples of practical effects. Giant props that make actors look extra small are also examples. The effect is then captured by the camera.

Computers were initially used in films to create motion-control effects. Mounting a camera on a track and controlling it with a computer helped filmmakers create certain effects. For example, if the camera were to move past a model vehicle, this would create the illusion on film that the vehicle is moving past the viewer. This process is considered a practical effect because a physical model is used.

Practical effects are great, but they do have drawbacks:

- A skilled **matte painter** could create a realistic background for a scene. But it would not be possible to move around in that background.

- Masks and **prosthetics** can be used to make a human look like a monster, but the human's proportions couldn't really change. So the effect sometimes doesn't look real enough to an audience. All they see is a person in a monster suit.

- Realistic **sets** of space stations or spacecrafts can be built. But such sets require huge sound stages, hundreds of construction experts, and the time to build them.

This effects artist creates a realistic miniature set.

Blink and Miss It

Live-action movies made before the 1980s did not contain more than a few seconds of **computer graphics** or **animation**.

The Need for a New Approach

Filmmaking became more advanced over time. Audiences expected more spectacular effects and visuals in films. Practical effects were becoming too expensive to create, and their limitations held back directors' visions.

Filmmakers searched for new ways to achieve their goals. They needed methods to create amazing effects without busting their budgets. Computers became more and more appealing.

Computer graphics started to be used in a few science fiction films in the 1970s. Movies such as *Star Wars*, *Alien*, and *Westworld* each contained a few seconds of CGI. CGI made fantastical things real—such as showing the world through a robotic character's machine eyes.

There was a revolution taking place behind the scenes in the film industry. Filmmakers, artists, and animators were testing computers to see what they could do to enhance films. What they created blew the minds of theater audiences.

Renaissance Geek

Dan O'Bannon, one of the screenwriters of *Alien*, was hired to produce graphics for the interior sets of the *Nostromo*, which is the spacecraft where all the movie's action takes place.

3:58 / 11:24

creature from *Alien*

Brave New World

Modern computers were originally built to solve complex math problems. At first, punch cards were used to **input** information. As technology advanced, computers could handle new and different tasks. They also became easier for people to use.

In 1972, computer scientists Ed Catmull and Fred Parke produced the first computer animation. They turned a cast of Catmull's hand into a series of polygons. The endpoints of the polygons were **digitized** by a computer to form the hand shape. Catmull and Parke wrote software that allowed the polygons to be bent and moved. The result was an animated hand that looked and moved like a real hand. By today's standards, this first animation was **crude**. But it was an important breakthrough that led to the field of computer graphics.

Soon after, short animations were created by universities around the world. They wanted to test the limits and capabilities of computers. Artists eagerly explored the new possibilities.

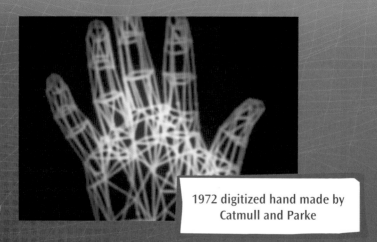

1972 digitized hand made by Catmull and Parke

From Pixels to Pixar

Ed Catmull went on to cofound Pixar, a company that specializes in computer-animated films such as *Toy Story* and *The Incredibles*.

Characters 101

Catmull and Parke's hand animation inspired artists and computer programmers everywhere. Is it possible to create characters and animations so realistic that they can pass for living things? It is—and here's how.

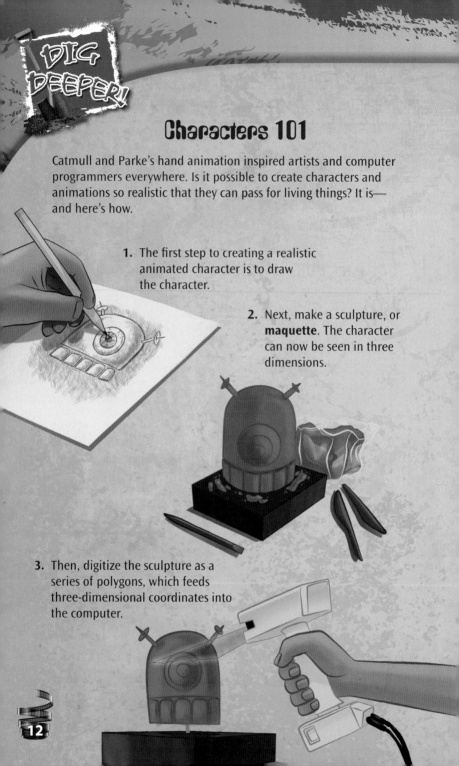

1. The first step to creating a realistic animated character is to draw the character.

2. Next, make a sculpture, or **maquette**. The character can now be seen in three dimensions.

3. Then, digitize the sculpture as a series of polygons, which feeds three-dimensional coordinates into the computer.

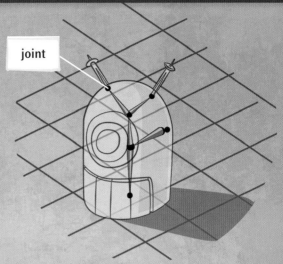

joint

4. The character can be built around a virtual **armature** so that its joints can bend and flex.

5. The armature can be covered with a texture. For example, a monster eye might need a glossy texture.

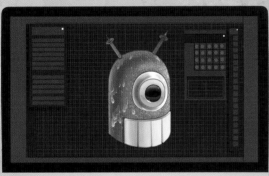

Fun with Polygons

Very complicated shapes can be created by joining polygons together. Once the shape is created, the polygon edges can be smoothed, resulting in a realistic object, such as an adventure setting in a video game.

A Breakthrough in Special Effects

In 1982, the Walt Disney film *Tron* was one of the first films to use CGI and animation as a setting for a story. *Tron* is the story of a video game designer who is transported into one of his games. He becomes trapped in battles against other programs. He must cross a digital desert to return to the real world. Sleek lightcycles, battle tanks, and solar ships carry programs over polygon landscapes.

The film only contains about twenty minutes of computer animation. And that was plenty! Audiences went wild for the crazy shapes and colors of *Tron*'s world. *Tron* showed that CGI effects could add new excitement to movies, and it paved the way for even more exciting things to come.

"Rapid Fire"

The amazing "bullet time" effects in *The Matrix*, which show time and motion dramatically slowed, were accomplished through computers. A rapid series of photos were taken on cameras placed around the actor. A computer stitched together the photos to make an exciting, mind-bending effect.

3:58 / 11:24

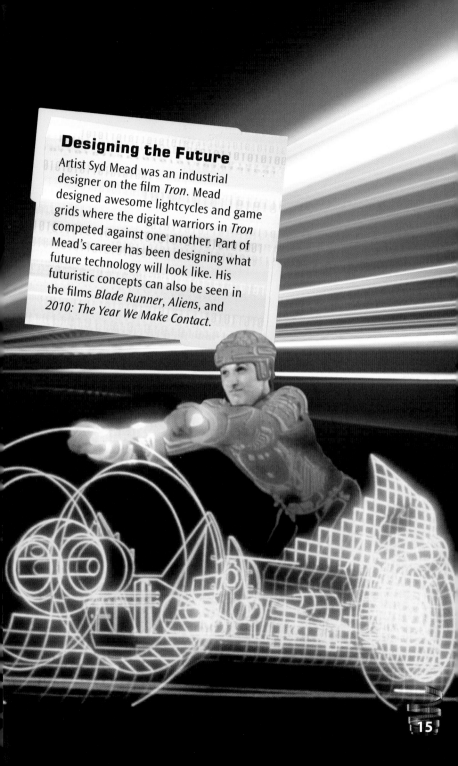

Designing the Future

Artist Syd Mead was an industrial designer on the film *Tron*. Mead designed awesome lightcycles and game grids where the digital warriors in *Tron* competed against one another. Part of Mead's career has been designing what future technology will look like. His futuristic concepts can also be seen in the films *Blade Runner*, *Aliens*, and *2010: The Year We Make Contact*.

Man of Iron

The film *The Iron Giant* is based on a 1968 book by Ted Hughes called *The Iron Man*. To keep it from being confused with the Marvel® superhero Iron Man®, the name of the movie was changed to *The Iron Giant*.

Blurring the Lines

Film directors began to see that computers could be effective tools to create amazing effects. They could help take movies to new levels of excitement and artistry.

The 1999 animated film *The Iron Giant* was made with traditional **cel animation**. Cel animation involves creating thousands of drawings of the characters by hand. Those drawings are hand-painted onto clear plastic sheets and then photographed. The brain sees a smooth, lifelike motion when the drawings are shown rapidly in order. Cel animation works well for human and animal characters. Objects such as cars or robots are more difficult to animate. Any wrong proportions on them are easy to spot.

The robot character in *The Iron Giant* was created with a computer. But the computer graphics copied the look of the film's cel animation. The result is that the robot fits well with the look of the film. Also, the robot's proportions are always correct.

It Began with a Mouse

Walt Disney and his studio are often credited with advancing the art of cel animation. In 1937, the studio released the first full-length animated cartoon, *Snow White and the Seven Dwarfs*. The film's realistic animation set the standard for cel animation, and it is considered a masterpiece, even by today's standards.

3:58 / 11:

Advancing the Art

The Iron Giant certainly wasn't the first huge metal man to appear on film, nor will he be the last. Giant robots have long been seen in movies and on television. There are also other movies that use both computer graphics and hand-drawn animation. In *Neon Genesis Evangelion*, robots defend Earth as alien monsters try to wipe out life. Humans control the robots.

This show first appeared as a television series in Japan in 1995. In 2008, several Evangelion films were made. The visuals were created using computer graphics. The animation in the films matches the style of the series. More detail and interest were added to the robots and effects through CGI.

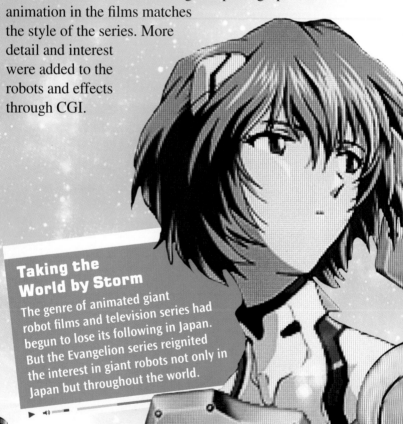

Taking the World by Storm

The genre of animated giant robot films and television series had begun to lose its following in Japan. But the Evangelion series reignited the interest in giant robots not only in Japan but throughout the world.

Anime

Neon Genesis Evangelion is an example of **anime**, a popular style of animation from Japan that is meant for children and adults. It is often characterized by colorful, highly **stylized**, and futuristic images.

The Pixar Revolution

Pixar started as a small group of digital artists. Their goal was to make the first animated film created solely with computers.

At first, the Pixar staff worked for Lucasfilm Ltd., the company that produced the Star Wars movies. They worked on special effects for a division called Industrial Light & Magic (ILM). This division was started in the 1970s to create practical and digital special effects for films. Pixar grew and soon became a separate company. In addition to creating special effects, Pixar also built its own line of computers. Some of those machines were sold to the Walt Disney Company. Pixar later developed a partnership with Disney to distribute its films. In 2006, Disney announced its plan to buy Pixar.

Toy Story

Pixar created the first fully CGI animated film. *Toy Story* debuted in 1995 to huge excitement. It is visually a different kind of film than had been seen before. The world of *Toy Story* is highly stylized. Toys are the main characters, but they are even more colorful and inviting than in real life.

The Incredibles

Pixar's 2004 film *The Incredibles* is also computer generated. The characters and settings are stylized, too, but in a very different way from those in *Toy Story*. There is an authenticity to the graphics. The story follows a family of superheroes who have given up using their powers. Audiences went wild over the action, humor, and heart in the story.

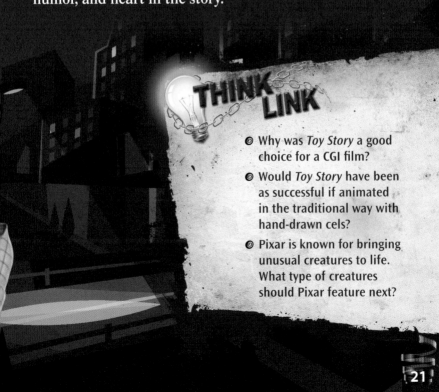

THINK LINK

- Why was *Toy Story* a good choice for a CGI film?
- Would *Toy Story* have been as successful if animated in the traditional way with hand-drawn cels?
- Pixar is known for bringing unusual creatures to life. What type of creatures should Pixar feature next?

The Race into Space

Depicting convincing special effects for science fiction films was a problem before computers. Spacecraft models were hung from wires in front of painted backgrounds or black curtains pierced with tiny holes like stars. The spacecraft might fly on a slightly visible wire. Those old effects couldn't meet audience demands for realism.

When a new crop of creative artists armed with computers got to work, they blasted sci-fi fans into space and beyond with out-of-this-world visuals.

KHAAAAAAAAAAAAAAAN!

Khan was first seen in the original Star Trek television series in 1967. This series used practical effects. In the 1982 film *Star Trek II: The Wrath of Khan*, growing animation technology created the effects. In the reboot film, *Star Trek: Into Darkness*, Khan returns with a huge space battleship, and an epic space battle ensues—only possible through today's CGI.

3:58 / 11:24

A New Frontier

The original *Star Trek* television series ran from 1966 to 1969. The series follows the captain and crew of the U.S.S. *Enterprise* as they explore the galaxy. The show was popular with viewers and continues in reruns today.

Fans remained excited about *Star Trek* after it was cancelled. So, Paramount Pictures made several feature films based on the series. The 1982 film *Star Trek II: The Wrath of Khan* features an impactful visual scene, made possible through CGI. In it, Admiral James T. Kirk watches a video which shows a machine that can rapidly remake a planet, creating life. But it also destroys any creatures already there. The **cutting-edge** scene was created by a small group at ILM. It was the same group that would later become Pixar.

The Star Wars films are known for creating cutting-edge special effects. These effects have been imitated throughout the film industry. ILM was founded by the creator of the Star Wars empire, George Lucas. He started the company to create the effects he wanted for his series.

In 1999, *Star Wars: Episode I—The Phantom Menace* features a desert race. The racers drive an array of pods powered by huge rocket engines. The pod-race scene combines live characters with CGI characters and vehicles. The high-speed race through canyons and over rock-filled plains is a fan favorite from the film and considered a masterwork of CGI.

Dinosaur Input Device

To create its impressive dinosaurs, the makers of *Jurassic Park* developed the Dinosaur (or Direct) Input Device (DID). The DID uses an armature covered in sensors to monitor the movements of the joints. The data is sent to a computer to create the animation.

The 1997 film *Starship Troopers* is based on the 1959 science fiction novel of the same name. In both, space soldiers battle a deadly army of alien insects attacking Earth.

Tippett Studios created and animated the alien bugs in *Starship Troopers*. Phil Tippett, the studio's founder, began his career as a stop-motion animator. But for *Starship Troopers*, his studio created a new method. Tippett animated the bugs to swarm the soldiers' base. First, a metal armature was made. Then, the armature was connected to a computer that recorded its movements. Those motions could then be applied to the swarming bugs.

scene from *Starship Troopers*

Power to the People

Advancements in computers happen very quickly. Computer hardware and software can do much more today than they could do a few years ago. Today's computers are much smaller and faster than they used to be just a decade ago. (The first modern computers filled entire rooms!)

Home Computer Revolution

Today, the power to produce amazing images and animations is available to everyone. Directors and animators have pushed the limits of creativity. They can now create feature films using only personal computers. You may be doing your homework on one of the same machines that made your favorite movie!

In 1994, director Kerry Conran began working on a film. He made it entirely on his home computer. Four years later, he was able to put human actors into completely CGI backgrounds. The six-minute piece was enough for Conran to receive funding to make the entire film. The sets and backgrounds of the finished movie were as strong as those created in studios.

Conran developed a unique approach for moviemaking. He used technology to achieve his vision. His 2004 film *Sky Captain and the World of Tomorrow* is filled with giant robots, airships, and a mad scientist. Conran created a fantastic futuristic adventure.

robot from *Sky Captain and the World of Tomorrow*

Do-It-Yourself

Many of the first workable home computers were delivered in kit form. Buyers had to build the computers.

Gareth Edwards used a slightly different approach when he wrote and directed the 2010 film *Monsters*. The story follows a reporter who accompanies his boss's daughter home through an "infected" zone. The zone is an area in Mexico that has been taken over by alien creatures. The aliens were brought to Earth by a NASA space **probe**. Huge creatures are everywhere as the pair crosses the infected zone. But are the aliens *really* dangerous bloodthirsty creatures? Or are they just misunderstood beings stranded on Earth?

Then and Now

Edwards claimed, "You can go in the shop now and you can buy a laptop that's faster than the computers they made *Jurassic Park* on."

The film was relatively inexpensive to make but was a surprise hit at theaters. Edwards produced all the special effects himself on his home computer. His do-it-yourself special effects allowed him enormous amounts of creativity. It also helped open the door for other filmmakers to take the same approach.

illustration inspired by 2010 movie *Monsters*

STOP! THINK...

- Compare and contrast the sizes of the monster, the humans, and the landscape.
- If this were a live-action movie, what CGI might be used to create this scene?
- How might you use CGI to change the landscape?

Virtually Real

As computers advanced, digital effects enabled filmmakers to make giant leaps forward in realism. Backgrounds could be more highly detailed, and hair and fur could look realistic. CGI characters started to appear on movie and television screens more often. The more believable these characters were as humans, the more audiences forgot that CGI wasn't real.

Examples of great CGI are easy to find. Here's a walk through some of the best and most significant examples of CGI magic.

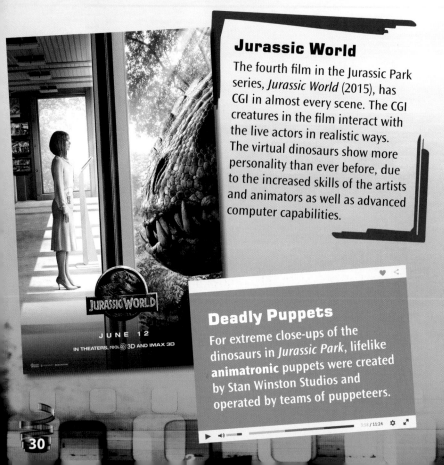

Jurassic World

The fourth film in the Jurassic Park series, *Jurassic World* (2015), has CGI in almost every scene. The CGI creatures in the film interact with the live actors in realistic ways. The virtual dinosaurs show more personality than ever before, due to the increased skills of the artists and animators as well as advanced computer capabilities.

Deadly Puppets

For extreme close-ups of the dinosaurs in *Jurassic Park*, lifelike **animatronic** puppets were created by Stan Winston Studios and operated by teams of puppeteers.

Jurassic Park (1993)

The most frustrating thing about dinosaurs is that they aren't around anymore. However, computer advances have made it seem as if they are. In 1993, the film *Jurassic Park* showed audiences why it's better that dinosaurs *aren't* around! Jurassic Park is an amusement theme park filled with live dinosaurs that were bred from ancient DNA. As often happens in adventure movies, *things go horribly wrong*. An employee shuts down the park's security system. The dinosaurs escape and cause panic and chaos for the staff.

There is actually a very small amount of CGI footage in *Jurassic Park*. But it was enough to pave the way for future films to bring the nonexistent to life.

The Abyss (1989)

James Cameron wrote and directed an undersea science fiction film called *The Abyss*. The crew of a deep-sea oil platform finds an alien colony on the ocean floor. One CGI effect shows an alien water tentacle reaching inside the platform. That one sequence, containing just over a minute of CGI, took seven special effects groups six months to complete!

Terminator 2: Judgment Day

Cameron used the water tentacle effect again in a dramatic way in his 1991 film *Terminator 2: Judgment Day*. A robot is made from material called "liquid metal." Through CGI, the metal can reshape itself into almost any form and repair itself after severe damage.

3:58 / 11:24

Original Alien Invasion

War of the Worlds by H. G. Wells was published as a novel in 1898. The story centers on a character who finds himself in the midst of an alien invasion in London. A radio teleplay of the story was broadcast in 1938. Many listeners tuned in late, missing the **disclaimer** that it was not a real invasion. Some people began to panic, believing the story was real!

War of the Worlds (2005)

A remake of the classic 1953 movie *War of the Worlds* has the benefit of modern special effects. Scenes of an Earth invasion, walking machines, and creepy Martians were made believable through CGI. The earlier version of the film used cutting-edge models to portray the Martians. It was hailed as a great film in its time. But the comparison between the two versions shows just how far technology has advanced.

Star Trek (2009) and *Star Trek: Into Darkness* (2013)

Director J. J. Abrams launched a reboot of the original Star Trek. He made full use of modern CGI to update Star Trek for a new audience. The stories in the newer films have the humor and action the original show is known for. But they also include eye-popping space battles, alien creatures, and wonders in space.

Star Trek

An updated version of the 1960s Star Trek series was released on DVD in 2007. New special effects were added that enhanced the original shows. All the spacecraft and alien planet scenes were redone to make them more realistic. More color and motion were added to painted backgrounds. Even stains in the uniforms worn on the show were hidden!

CGI on a Big Scale

James Cameron's movie *Avatar* was done with about 70 percent CGI. It also used a breakthrough technique called image-based facial performance capture. For *Avatar*, this technique was used mainly on the actors' faces. For this to work, an actor wears a custom-fit helmet with a small boom pole attached. At the end of the pole is a camera that is set directly in front of the actor's face. This camera records every facial and eye movement and sends the information to a computer. The result is a character with more realistic human expressions.

Inception (2010)

It makes sense to think that as technology links the planet, criminals will find weaknesses in that technology. The film *Inception* follows a crew of high-tech thieves who break into their targets' dreams. One of the thieves finds out the hard way that sometimes dreams can turn on you.

Director Christopher Nolan used CGI to show how the dream world is manipulated. City blocks fold over on themselves, bridges rise from the ground, and staircases lead back to themselves. *Inception* is a twisted mystery with layers of dream imagery that take audiences on a dizzying chase.

Interstellar (2014)

While *Inception* journeys into the human mind, Nolan's *Interstellar* journeys deep into space. The film follows the crew of a space mission to find a new home for humans stuck on a dying Earth. Livable planets are seen through a wormhole. Among the CGI effects are planets with massive tidal waves and frozen clouds. An astronaut even gets trapped in 5-D space!

What Does a Black Hole Look Like?

Nolan was advised by a Caltech physicist on how a black hole might appear if you were able to get close enough to take a good look.

5:58 / 11:24

An Artist and Director

Director Ridley Scott is also a talented artist. He generates hundreds of sketches and **storyboards** to help the crew understand what he envisions for his films.

Gravity (2013)

Director Alfonso Cuarón's film *Gravity* is about astronauts stranded in space after a debris storm severely damages their shuttle. A unique combination of filming and CGI was used to recreate the setting of outer space.

Many of the scenes are entirely CGI except for the actors' faces. For other scenes, the challenge of the film was achieving the look of a zero gravity environment. To do this, Cuarón worked with a talented special effects team and collaborated with NASA. Their hard work paid off—the film won an Academy Award® for Best Achievement in Visual Effects.

Green-Screen Effects

Using the green-screen technique allows filmmakers to create scenes without building sets. A stage is painted green or draped in green fabric, and live actors are filmed against the green color. Separately, a "virtual" set is made with CGI. The virtual set is combined digitally with the live-actor footage, with the green color replaced by the virtual sets.

Dreams of a CGI Future

The year: 1962
The place: home of Ray Harryhausen, master of stop-motion animation effects

Harryhausen works late into the night on what will become his favorite film: *Jason and the Argonauts*.

Stop-motion animation involves tiny movements of a model. The viewer's brain perceives the separate movements as a continuous motion!

click

click

click

click

click

yawn...
There has to be an easier way to do this!

Harryhausen grows fatigued from the **Herculean** task.

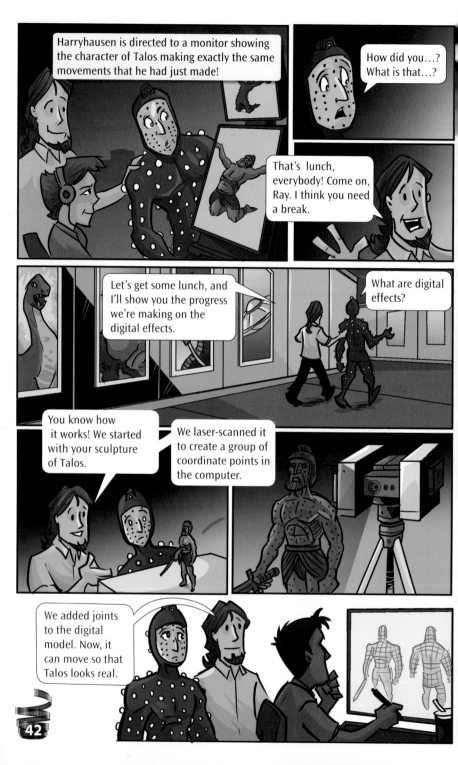

Motion Capture in Action

The most difficult task for a director may be to create realistic fantasy creatures that audiences will believe exist. Part of the director's challenge is to make unique shapes and textures for these beings. The other more difficult part is to animate the character in a realistic way.

Motion capture does this. The major skeletal joints of an actor are marked with reflectors. The actor then performs a scene while a digital camera records it. The recording is then run through software. The computer identifies the movements of the markers on the actor. Then it applies those movements to a CGI character. The animated character takes the place of the live-motion performer.

a full body suit designed specifically for human motion capture

Gollum

Actor Andy Serkis played the completely computer-generated character Gollum from *The Hobbit: An Unexpected Journey* and the Lord of the Rings trilogy films, directed by Peter Jackson. Motion capture made it possible. For close-ups of Gollum's face, a small video camera recorded Serkis's facial expressions to introduce the amazingly subtle and realistic character to audiences.

Sonny from *I, Robot*

In 2004, a film based loosely on Isaac Asimov's classic book *I, Robot* debuted. In it, a police detective works to discover who (or what) is guilty of murder. The film's success centers on presenting a realistic robot. Motion capture proved to be the ideal technique to create Sonny, the accused robot. Actor Alan Tudyk makes Sonny a complex and sympathetic character. The film strongly portrays a world full of humanoid robots.

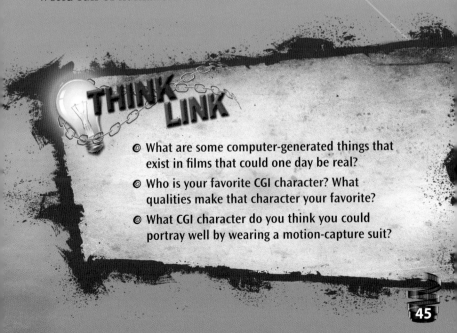

THINK LINK

- ◎ What are some computer-generated things that exist in films that could one day be real?
- ◎ Who is your favorite CGI character? What qualities make that character your favorite?
- ◎ What CGI character do you think you could portray well by wearing a motion-capture suit?

King Kong (1933)

King Kong has been redone many times since the original stop-motion masterpiece. The challenge for each film has been to create a convincing giant ape. Oversized puppets, men in ape suits, or other giant props have never been realistic enough for audiences to accept.

In 2005, director Peter Jackson tackled a modern retelling of the Kong story. He used cutting-edge CGI to help audiences **suspend their disbelief**. Jackson worked with actor Andy Serkis to create the ape. Computer-graphic artists were able to take his work and apply it to the realistic Kong character. The ape seems almost human.

Andy Serkis: The Future of Acting

Actor and voiceover artist Andy Serkis is one of the most experienced motion-capture actors working today. He has founded his own motion-capture studio, The Imaginarium Studios.

5:38 / 11:24

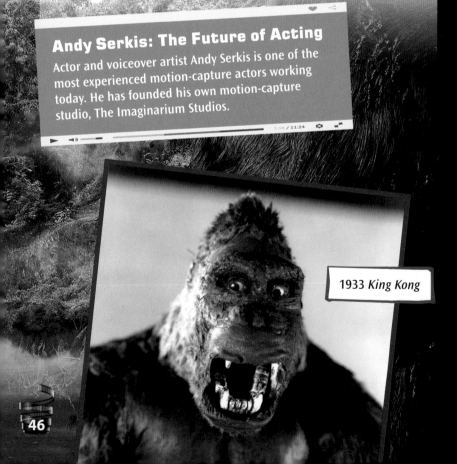

1933 *King Kong*

2005 *King Kong*

Rise of the Planet of the Apes (2011)

The original Planet of the Apes films of the late 1960s and '70s feature a planet where apes are intelligent and humans are wild. The apes are actors with makeup and prosthetics. This approach was realistic for the time. Audiences flocked to see each film.

In 2011, this franchise was rebooted. Peter Jackson's visual effects company helped create this movie. More realistic apes were made by using the visual effects techniques from 2005's *King Kong*. Andy Serkis portrays the lead ape character. The apes are not only lifelike but also sympathetic. After watching the film for a few moments, it is easy to forget that the apes began as a series of **pixels** on a computer.

Motion Capture DIY

With the right software and hardware, anyone can create a spine-tingling digital monster. It's as easy as one, two, three!

1. Get a great actor to wear a motion-capture suit.
2. Apply the motion-capture performance to the digital character.
3. Enjoy the finished result with a digital character in your film!

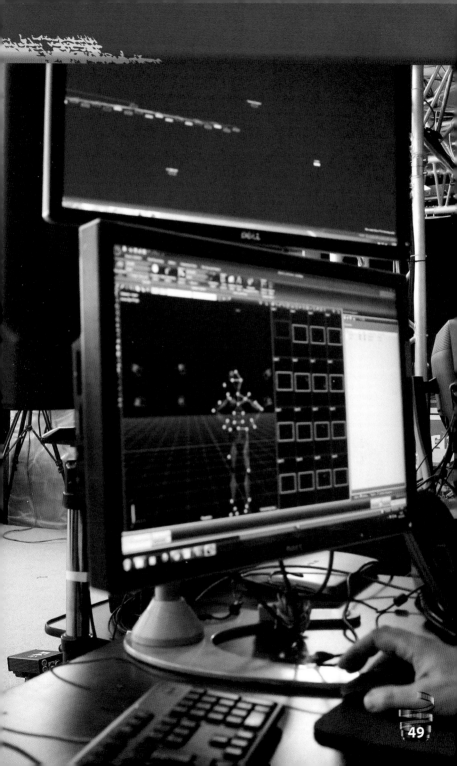

Virtual Visionaries

Computers weren't designed for the purpose of making art. A few creative visionaries have explored and tested the ways computers can be used. They have set the stage for dynamic CGI and animation.

Walt Disney

Walt Disney encouraged new ways to think about hand-drawn animation. Disney and his animators created the first cel-animated feature-length film in 1937. *Snow White and the Seven Dwarfs* was a huge hit.

Ed Catmull

Ed Catmull is a computer expert who saw that computers could be used in creating animations. He developed new approaches in computer graphics and digital filmmaking. In 1972, his CGI hand animation was a leap forward.

George Lucas made the first *Star Wars* film in 1977. He knew that he would need new approaches to create the right effects for his films. He founded Industrial Light & Magic to create the effects and to pioneer the use of CGI.

George Lucas

Stephen Lisberger's use of computer graphics started in the late 1970s. He created a studio to make films that used computer graphics. His short film of the character Tron led to innovative ways of making movies.

Stephen Lisberger

James Cameron wanted to find new technologies to create realistic special effects. One scene in his 1989 film *The Abyss* called for a "tentacle" of water to reach into an undersea base. It took Cameron six months to produce the final sequence. The scene ran for just over a minute!

James Cameron

Phil Tippett followed in the footsteps of Ray Harryhausen in creating stop motion. *Jurassic Park* director Steven Spielberg decided to create dinosaurs through CGI. Tippett was the right artist to merge stop motion with digital animation.

Phil Tippett

John Lasseter was an animator for the Walt Disney Company. He preferred to use CGI instead of cel animation and got hired at Lucasfilm. He managed a department that would ultimately become Pixar.

John Lasseter

For their film *The Matrix*, the Wachowskis needed an effect that froze time. To create it, cameras were arranged around an actor as he moved. A computer blended the photos into an animation.

The Wachowskis

14

Peter Jackson's Lord of the Rings trilogy features the first use of motion capture. Actor Andy Serkis wore a costume that allowed his movements to be recorded. Those movements were then used to animate the CGI character of Gollum.

Peter Jackson

Kerry Conran devised a technique for using live actors but with completely CGI sets and backgrounds. *Sky Captain and the World of Tomorrow* was the first film to be created in this new way.

Kerry Conran

In Alfonso Cuarón's film *Gravity*, nearly all the scenes were computer generated. The live actors were filmed separately. Computers were used to create the effects. They were also used to join together the individual effect shots.

Alfonso Cuarón

What's Coming Next?

We have seen some remarkable advances in the special effects used in film and television over the last few decades. Film directors are at a point where their most wild and creative visions can be captured and projected onto screens in convincing ways. What will they do next? What's the next step after realism has been achieved?

You can bet that computer technology will continue to advance and introduce faster and less-expensive shortcuts for CGI. For example, 3-D printers are making it possible to craft suits of "armor" and other costume pieces. First, a body scan of an actor can be recorded on a computer. Then, a computer-generated costume can be sent to a 3-D printer for fabrication. This method simplifies the traditional process. At one time, actors had to have full-body plaster casts made to make armor. This was an arduous process for the actors. It was also quite a challenge for the artists and animators who made the prosthetics from the casts.

The End of Actors?

As advances are made in CGI, some actors worry that computerized characters will replace human actors. The art of acting has been around since ancient times and is enjoyed in many formats. It seems unlikely that actors will ever be replaced. In fact, they're at the heart of some of the best CGI!

3:58 / 11:24

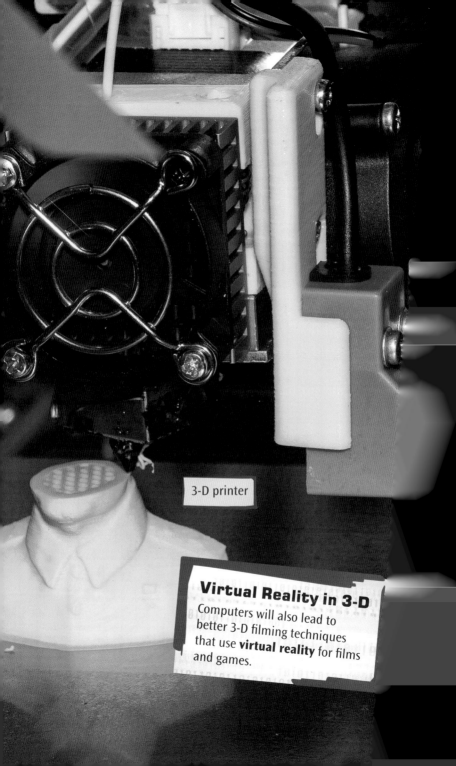

3-D printer

Virtual Reality in 3-D
Computers will also lead to better 3-D filming techniques that use **virtual reality** for films and games.

Advances in computer technology will also enable new generations to create stunning visuals. All they'll need are modest computers to produce amazing effects. And it'll cost a fraction of what it costs now. Experts keep squeezing more capabilities into smaller chips and machines. Lower prices have a way of freeing creativity! They allow a forum for the seemingly impossible to become real.

The next breakthroughs in CGI may be as unknown to us as the motion capture used in the newest *King Kong* would have been back in 1933. Perhaps the most important part of the next advances in special effects will be how they make possible a renewed focus on the script and characters. The best visuals support the film rather than steal the spotlight from the characters and the story. Audiences may no longer go to the movies to check out its special effects—they will be there to watch a great story unfold!

CGI on a Big Scale

CGI is becoming so detailed that it is increasingly more difficult to tell what's real. Take a look at these two images. Can you tell which eye is CGI?

Living Forever

CGI has made it possible to include actors who have died during the production of new films. When actor Paul Walker died during the filming of his last movie, CGI as well as a body double were combined to include him in new scenes.

Glossary

animation—a way of making movies with a series of drawings, constructed figures, or computer-generated images

animatronic—electronically controlled robot

anime—a style of animation created in Japan that uses bold colors and stylized characters

armature—an internal "skeleton" inside a sculpture or robot

cel animation—an art technique where paintings on separate sheets of clear acetate (cels) are shown rapidly one after another, creating the illusion of movement

computer graphics—pictures, shapes, and words produced by a computer

cosmos—the universe and all the astronomical bodies within it

crude—very simple and basic, showing minimal skill and craftmanship

cutting-edge—the most advanced; the newest thing

digitized—turned a shape into computer coordinates

disclaimer—a statement made to avoid misunderstanding

hardware—computer equipment

Herculean—related to extraordinary intensity

input—to feed information into a computer

live-action movies—movies made with real people and places

maquette—a small sculpture, used to digitize a character into a computer

matte painter—an artist who specializes in painting backgrounds used in practical effects shots in films

pixels—very small dots that form a picture on a screen

practical effects—effects filmed using models or other figures and then filmed by a camera

probe—a spaceship sent into space to explore and collect data

prosthetics—artificial body parts or features used to change an actor's face or body

release—the launch of a movie for the public to see

sets—constructed environments where movie scenes are filmed

software—the programs that run on computers to perform specific functions

special effects—images or sounds created for a movie to suggest something real

storyboards—side-by-side drawings that show the events of stories in sequence

stylized—having exaggerated features or proportions

suspend their disbelief—let go of the reality people think they know

valiant—very brave

virtual reality—false images created to suggest reality, often seen through special headsets, glasses, or on screen

Index

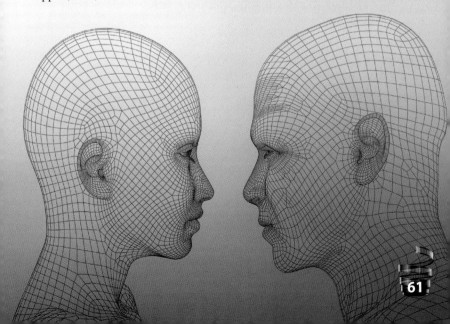

Check It Out!

Books

Asimov, Isaac. 2008. *I, Robot*. Spectra.

Byrne, Bill. 2009. *Movie Maker: The Visual Effects Arsenal: VFX Solutions for the Independent Filmmaker*. Focal Press.

Failes, Ian. 2015. *Masters of FX: Behind the Scenes with Geniuses of Visual and Special Effects*. Focal Press.

Grabham, Tim, Suridh Hassan, Dave Reeve, and Clare Richards. 2010 *Movie Maker: The Ultimate Guide to Making Films*. Candlewick Press.

Sawicki, Mark. 2011. *Filming the Fantastic: A Guide to Visual Effects Cinematography*. Focal Press.

Wells, H. G. 2012. *War of the Worlds*. Tribeca Books.

Videos

I, Robot. Alex Proyas. 2004. Twentieth Century Fox.

War of the Worlds. Steven Spielberg. 2005. Paramount Pictures.

Websites

Pixar. http://www.pixar.com.

Try It!

For an upcoming interview with a prestigious film studio, you must make a short film (3 to 5 minutes) to display your work. It can be an animated film, one using people (friends or family), or other objects (building blocks, clay figures, etc.).

- First, draw a storyboard.

- Write a script if characters will be speaking.

- Gather all the materials necessary for the film.

- Create or design the set depending on what type of movie you're producing. You may also need costumes.

- Rehearse the story several times, making sure everyone involved knows what to do and say.

- Record your movie. Invite others to watch your production.

About the Author

Tim Bradley grew up watching films loaded with special effects. He would constantly draw spaceships and aliens, and had so much fun that he decided to do it for a living! As a professional artist and author, Tim writes about the wild stuff of science and science fiction. Tim lives in sunny Southern California with his wife and son.